A PURRFECT LIFE

42 Illustrated Tips for Your Cat's Happy and Healthy Life

Deepak Panickal & Tina Joseph

DEDICATION

To our beloved furball, Mollykutty*!
Thanks for sprinkling your magic on these pages.
You're the heart and soul of this book!

* The Malayalam word "kutty" typically translates to "small" or "little" in English. It is often used to describe something or someone of small size or stature, and is also used as an endearing term to refer to a child or a loved one.

CONTENTS

Chapter 1

Setting Up & Essentials

01

Kitten-proof your home

Secure Hazardous Items

- Tuck away electrical cords and wires to prevent chewing, which can pose a risk of electrocution or injury.
- Identify and remove any toxic plants from your home, as ingestion can lead to serious health issues for kittens.
- Store cleaning supplies and chemicals in locked cabinets or high shelves to prevent accidental ingestion or exposure.

Protect Fragile Objects

- Secure fragile items such as vases, glassware, and ornaments to prevent them from being knocked over or broken by curious kittens.
- Place valuable or delicate items out of reach on higher surfaces or behind closed doors to minimize the risk of damage.
- Consider using childproof locks or barriers to restrict access to areas with breakable objects or decorations.

Supervise and Monitor

- Supervise your kitten closely, especially in unfamiliar areas or during exploratory play.
- Monitor their behaviour and interactions with household items, intervening to prevent accidents or mishaps.
- Provide plenty of safe and stimulating toys and activities to redirect your kitten's energy and curiosity away from potential hazards.

02

The right litter box

Litter box

Size and Accessibility

- Select a litter box that is spacious enough for your cat to comfortably turn around and dig.
- A covered box can provide privacy and reduce litter scatter, but ensure it's large enough for your cat to stretch comfortably.
- Accessibility is key, especially for kittens or senior cats, so choose a box with low entry points for easy access.

Covered or Uncovered Options

- Covered litter boxes offer privacy and help contain odours, but some cats may prefer uncovered boxes for easier entry and exit.
- Uncovered boxes allow for better airflow and visibility, which can be beneficial for cats who are sensitive to confined spaces.

Maintenance and Hygiene

- Regularly scoop and clean the litter box to maintain cleanliness and prevent odours.
- Consider using liners or mats to make cleaning easier and reduce litter tracking.
- Place the litter box in a quiet, low-traffic area of your home to provide a safe and comfortable environment for your cat.

03

The perfect litter

Unscented Clumping Clay

- Start with unscented clumping clay litter as it's familiar to most cats and offers easy maintenance.
- Clumping litter forms solid clumps when wet, making it easier to scoop and maintain cleanliness in the litter box.
- Unscented litter avoids overwhelming your cat with artificial fragrances, which can be off-putting or irritating to their sensitive sense of smell.

Experiment with Varieties

- Once your cat is accustomed to the litter box, consider experimenting with different litter types to find their preference.
- Options include silica gel crystals, natural wood, or corn-based litter, each offering unique benefits such as odour control or environmental friendliness.
- Observing your cat's behaviour and litter box habits can help determine which type of litter they prefer.

Transition Gradually

- Introduce new litter gradually by mixing small amounts with the familiar litter, increasing the proportion over time.
- Watch for any signs of aversion or discomfort during the transition and revert to the previous litter if necessary.

04

Comfortable bedding

Cozy Resting Space

- Offer a comfortable bed, crate, or soft blanket in a quiet corner of your home where your cat can relax undisturbed.
- Cats enjoy having a designated space to retreat to for rest and relaxation, away from noise and distractions.
- Providing a cozy bedding area helps your cat feel secure and promotes better sleep quality.

Heated Options

- Consider using a heated pad or bed to provide extra warmth and comfort, especially during colder months or for cats with arthritis.
- Heated bedding options mimic the warmth of a cat's natural sleeping environment, such as sunbathing spots or cozy laps.
- A simple solution that works is to drape a rug or towel over a radiator.

Maintenance and Hygiene

- Regularly clean and wash bedding to maintain hygiene and freshness, removing any accumulated fur and dirt.
- Monitor bedding for signs of wear or damage, replacing it as needed to ensure your cat's comfort and safety.

05

Food and water bowls

Non-Porous and Hygienic

- Opt for bowls made from ceramic or stainless steel, which are non-porous materials that are easy to clean and resistant to bacterial growth.

Location

- Place food and water bowls away from the litter box to prevent contamination of food and water with litter particles.
- Cats have a natural aversion to eating near their bathroom area, so separating the bowls helps prevent stress.
- Placing water bowls in a quiet, low-traffic area of your home encourages regular drinking habits.

Accessibility and Comfort

- Ensure food and water bowls are easily accessible to your cat, placed at a comfortable height and distance apart.
- Consider elevated bowls for older cats or those with mobility issues to reduce strain on their neck and joints while eating and drinking.

06

Scratch posts

Variety of Options

- Provide multiple scratch posts with various textures, such as carpet, cardboard, and sisal rope.
- Offering both vertical and horizontal scratching surfaces accommodates different scratching styles and allows your cat to stretch and exercise comfortably.
- Place scratch posts strategically, including in areas where your cat likes to relax or play, to encourage regular use.

Height and Stability

- Choose scratch posts that are tall enough for your cat to fully extend their body and sturdy enough to withstand vigorous scratching.
- Ensure that they are stable and securely anchored to prevent tipping or wobbling during use.

Encourage Proper Behaviour

- Regularly redirect your cat to the designated scratch posts whenever they attempt to scratch furniture or other inappropriate surfaces.
- Use treats or praise, to reward your cat for using the scratch posts appropriately.
- Catnip works as a great motivator when applied on scratch posts.

07

Interactive toys

Variety of Toys

- Offer a variety of interactive toys such as wands, feathers, and catnip-filled toys to engage different senses and instincts.
- Interactive toys encourage mental and physical stimulation, providing entertainment and exercise for your cat.
- Rotate toys regularly to keep playtime exciting and prevent boredom.

Puzzle Feeders

- Incorporate puzzle feeders into your cat's routine to stimulate their hunting instincts and provide mental stimulation.
- They encourage problem-solving skills as your cat works to retrieve food or treats from hidden compartments.
- Using puzzle feeders during meal times adds an element of fun and helps prevent over-eating by slowing down eating.

Supervised Play and Safety

- Always supervise your cat during playtime with toys to ensure their safety.
- Check toys regularly for signs of wear or damage, replacing them as needed to prevent ingestion of small parts.
- Interactive play strengthens the bond between you and your cat while promoting a happy and healthy lifestyle.

08

Carrier for safe travels

Comfortable and Secure

- Select a carrier that provides ample space for your cat to stand, turn around, and lie down comfortably.
- Opt for carriers with good build quality and secure latches to ensure your cat's safety.
- A carrier with good ventilation and easy access for loading and unloading your cat will make trips more comfortable for them.

Familiarization Process

- Introduce the carrier to your cat by leaving it open in a familiar, comfortable area of your home.
- Encourage your cat to explore the carrier by placing treats, toys, or bedding inside.
- Gradually increase the amount of time your cat spends in the carrier, rewarding calm behaviour and providing reassurance as needed.

Reduce Anxiety

- Familiarizing your cat with the carrier helps reduce anxiety associated with travel.
- Regularly using the carrier for short trips, even if not to the vet, reinforces positive associations and builds confidence.

09

Harness and leash training

Gradual Introduction

- Begin training in a calm, quiet environment indoors to help your cat acclimate to the harness and leash.
- Offer treats and praise, to associate the harness and leash with pleasant experiences.
- Gradually increase the duration of training sessions, allowing your cat to become comfortable wearing the harness and leash.

Proper Equipment

- Choose the right-sized harness that fits snugly but comfortably around your cat's body, with room for adjustment as they grow.
- Select a lightweight leash made from a durable material, such as nylon, for freedom of movement while maintaining control.
- Ensure the harness and leash are securely attached to prevent escape during outdoor excursions.

Safety First

- Supervise your cat closely during outdoor walks to monitor their behaviour and surroundings.
- Avoid crowded or noisy areas that may overwhelm or frighten your cat, and be prepared to return indoors if they show signs of distress.

10

Microchip and Collar

Identification

- A microchip or collar with an ID tag provides essential identification in case your cat gets lost.
- Include your contact information on the tag or microchip so that anyone who finds your cat can easily contact you.
- In the event of an unfortunate emergency, proper identification helps reunite you with your cat quickly.

Microchip

- Microchips offer a permanent form of identification that cannot be lost or removed, unlike a collar.
- Regularly update your contact information in the microchip when you change addresses to ensure accuracy.

Collar Safety

- Choose a collar that fits comfortably but securely around your cat's neck, allowing room for growth and movement.
- Get a detachable collar as it is a matter of safety in case the cat manages to get itself stuck.
- Supervise your cat initially when introducing a collar to ensure they adjust safely.

Chapter 2

Nutrition & Feeding

11

Age-specific food is essential

Proper Growth

- Kittens have unique nutritional needs to support their rapid growth and development.
- Age-appropriate kitten food is formulated with higher levels of protein, essential vitamins, and minerals crucial for healthy bone and muscle development.

Prevention of Health Issues

- Feeding adult cat food to kittens may lead to nutritional deficiencies or excesses.
- Age-specific food helps prevent issues like malnutrition or growth abnormalities, promoting overall well-being.
- Proper nutrition during kittenhood sets the foundation for a healthy adulthood, reducing the risk of health problems later in life.

Vet Consultation

- Consult your veterinarian to determine the best age-specific food based on the cat's breed, size, and health status.

12

Feeding schedule

Establish a Routine

- Set specific meal times for your cat and adhere to them every day.
- Consistent feeding times help regulate your cat's metabolism and prevent overeating or obesity.
- Establishing a routine also creates a sense of security and predictability for your cat, reducing stress.

Managing Availability

- If you're away for short periods, leave out dry food in a designated feeding area for your cat.
- Timed automatic feeders provides a convenient option for self-feeding and ensures your cat has access to nutrition throughout the day.

Monitor and Adjust

- Keep track of your cat's weight and body condition to ensure they're maintaining a healthy balance.
- Regularly evaluate your feeding schedule and adjust portion sizes or frequency as needed.

13

Fresh water

Importance of Hydration

- Cats require constant access to fresh water to stay hydrated and maintain proper bodily functions.
- Dehydration can lead to health issues such as urinary tract problems or kidney disease.
- Ensure your cat has a clean water source available at all times to promote optimal hydration.

Encouraging Consumption

- Cats are famous in being reluctant to drink, so consider investing in a water fountain to encourage drinking.
- Water fountains provide a constant flow of fresh water, which may entice your cat to drink more.
- Encouraging adequate water intake is crucial, especially for cats consuming dry food, to prevent health issues.

Regular Maintenance

- Keep the water bowl or fountain clean by washing it regularly with mild soap and water.
- Change the water daily to prevent bacteria buildup and ensure freshness.
- Monitoring your cat's water intake and habits can help you detect any potential health concerns early on.

14

Beware of table scraps

Resist Temptation

- Avoid giving in to the temptation to feed your cat scraps from the table.
- Human food may contain ingredients that are harmful to cats or disrupt their diet.
- Providing a balanced and nutritionally complete diet tailored to your cat's specific needs is essential for their overall health and well-being.

Prevent Bad Habits

- Feeding table scraps can lead to the development of bad habits such as begging or scavenging for food.
- Cats may become selective eaters, preferring human food over their designated meals.
- By sticking to their prescribed diet, you establish healthy eating habits and discourage undesirable behaviours in your kitten.

15

Gradual food transitions

Slow Transition Process

- Introduce the new food slowly over a period of about a month as a rough guidance.
- Start by mixing a small amount of the new food with the current food.
- Gradually increase the proportion of the new food while decreasing the old food to avoid digestive upset.

Prevent Digestive Issues

- Abrupt changes in diet can lead to gastrointestinal issues such as constipation or diarrhea.
- A slow transition allows your cat's digestive system to adapt slowly to the new food.

Observe

- Observe your cat's response to the new food, paying attention to any signs of digestive discomfort.

Chapter 3

Litter Box Training & Hygiene

16

Location, location, location

Quiet and Private Space

- Select a quiet area of your home away from high-traffic areas and noisy appliances.
- Cats prefer privacy when using the litter box, so choose a location where they feel secure and undisturbed.

Accessible and Convenient

- Ensure the litter box is easily accessible for your cat at all times, and doesn't accidently end up behind a closed door.
- Place it in a location that is convenient for both you as well so that it is easy to maintain and clean.

Stress-Free Environment

- Avoid placing the litter box near areas where your cat may feel anxious, such as near loud areas or next to exposed spaces.
- A peaceful and stress-free environment encourages your cat to use the litter box consistently and promotes their overall well-being.

17

Scoop it often

Regular Cleaning Routine

- Scoop the litter box at least once or twice daily to remove waste and maintain cleanliness.
- Every once in a while, empty out all the litter, and wash the litter box.

Encourage Usage

- Cats are more likely to use a clean litter box, so frequent scooping encourages consistent litter box habits.
- A clean litter box minimizes the risk of accidents.

Hygiene and Health

- Maintaining a clean litter box reduces the spread of bacteria and lowers the risk of urinary tract infections or other health issues.
- Regular cleaning also allows you to monitor your cat's litter box habits and quickly identify any changes or potential health concerns.

18

'Paw'sitive reinforcement is key

Encourage Desired Behaviour

- Use verbal praise, affectionate strokes, or small treats to reward your kitten when they use the litter box correctly.

Consistency is Key

- Be consistent in your efforts, praising your kitten each time they use the litter box appropriately.

Avoid Negative Interactions

- Refrain from scolding or punishing your kitten for accidents outside the litter box.
- Negative reinforcement can cause stress and anxiety, hindering training progress.

19

Patience is a virtue

Allow Time for Adjustment

- Understand that litter box training is a learning process for kittens, requiring patience and consistent praise.
- Give your kitten time to familiarize themselves with the litter box and its purpose, without expecting immediate results.

Manage Accidents with Grace

- Accidents are a normal part of the learning process, so remain patient and avoid scolding or punishing your kitten.
- Clean up accidents promptly using an enzymatic cleaner to remove odours and prevent re-marking.
- Most kittens grasp litter box training within a few weeks with consistent guidance and patience.

20

Monitor litter box habits

Pay Attention

- Regularly observe your cat's litter box usage, noting any changes in frequency, amount, or consistency of urine and faeces.
- Pay attention to any straining, difficulty urinating or defecating, or signs of discomfort.

Detecting Health Issues

- Changes in litter box habits may signal underlying health problems such as urinary tract infections, kidney issues, or gastrointestinal disorders.
- Promptly addressing any abnormalities in litter box behaviour can lead to early detection and treatment of potential illnesses.

Veterinary Advice

- If you notice significant changes in your cat's litter box habits or have concerns about their urinary or digestive health, consult your veterinarian as soon as possible.

Chapter 4

Socialization & Playtime

21

Handle your kitten often

Early Acclimatization

- Start handling your kitten gently and frequently from a young age to familiarize them with human touch.
- Gradually introduce different types of handling, such as being picked up, held, and petted, to get them used to various sensations.

Build Trust and Confidence

- Regular handling builds trust between you and your kitten, helping them feel secure and confident in your presence.
- Positive experiences with handling encourage a calm and relaxed demeanor, reducing anxiety and fearfulness.

Strengthen the Bond

- Handling sessions provide valuable bonding opportunities, strengthening the emotional connection between you and your kitten.
- Use such time to engage in gentle play, grooming, or cuddling.
- A well-handled kitten grows into a sociable and affectionate cat, enriching your relationship and enhancing their overall well-being.

22

Introduce new people gradually

Gradual Introduction

- Introduce new people to your cat gradually, starting with familiar faces and slowly expanding their social circle.
- Allow your kitten to approach new individuals at their own pace.
- Step by step exposure helps build confidence and reduces the likelihood of fear or aggression towards strangers.

Supervised Interactions

- Always supervise interactions between your cat and new people to ensure safety.
- Monitor your cat's body language for signs of stress or discomfort, and intervene if necessary to prevent any negative encounters.

Consistent Socialization

- Maintain regular socialization efforts throughout your cat's life to prevent fearfulness towards unfamiliar individuals.
- Incorporate treats during social interactions to create positive associations with new people.

23

Playtime is bonding time

Regular Play

- Schedule daily interactive play sessions to strengthen the bond with your cat.
- Engage in activities that mimic hunting behaviour, such as wand toys or laser pointers.
- Interactive play fosters trust and companionship while providing physical and mental stimulation.

Stimulation and Exercise

- Playtime serves as essential exercise for your cat, helping to maintain a healthy weight and prevent obesity.
- Stimulating play sessions satisfy your cat's instincts and alleviate boredom, reducing the likelihood of destructive behaviour.

Quality Time Together

- Use playtime as an opportunity to connect with your kitten on a deeper level and understand their personality.
- Bonding through play strengthens your relationship as their caregiver and 'paw'rent.

24

Rotate the toys

Introduce Variety

- Rotate toys regularly to prevent boredom and maintain your cat's interest in play sessions.
- Offer a mix of toys with different textures, shapes, and sounds to stimulate your cat's senses.

DIY Options

- Get creative with DIY toys using household items like cardboard boxes, paper bags, or crumpled-up paper.
- DIY toys provide inexpensive and eco-friendly options to enrich your cat's playtime experience.
- Supervise your cat with DIY toys to ensure safety and replace them if they become damaged or worn out.

Interactive Play

- Dedicate regular play sessions to bond with your cat and provide physical and mental stimulation.
- Engage your cat in interactive play by mimicking prey-like movements or using toys that encourage hunting behaviours.

25

Learn their body language

Ears, Tail, and Vocalizations

- Forward and relaxed ears indicate contentment, while flattened suggest fear or aggression.
- Upright tail position signals confidence, while tucked between legs may indicate anxiety.
- Purring usually signifies contentment, while hissing or growling may signal discomfort or aggression.

Mood Assessment

- Understand your cat's body language to gauge their emotional state and well-being.
- Recognize subtle cues like dilated pupils or a puffed-up tail, which may indicate stress or agitation.
- Getting familiarized to your cat's mood helps prevent misunderstandings.

Avoid Misinterpretation

- Avoid misinterpreting playful behaviours as aggression by paying attention to accompanying body language.
- Educate yourself on common cat signals to accurately discern your cat's intentions and feelings.

Chapter 5

Health & Wellness

26

Schedule regular vet checkups

First Vet Visit

- Schedule your kitten's first vet appointment within the first few weeks of bringing them home.
- This initial visit allows the vet to assess your kitten's health, address any concerns, prepare for spaying/neutering, and establish a baseline for future care.
- Early veterinary care sets the foundation for a lifetime of good health and ensures any potential issues are identified.

Follow Vaccination Schedule

- Follow your vet's recommended vaccination schedule to protect your cat against common infectious diseases.
- Adhering to the schedule ensures your cat receives timely protection and minimizes contracting preventable diseases.

Ongoing Checkups

- Maintain regular checkups as recommended by your veterinarian, typically every 6-12 months.
- Routine examinations allow the vet to monitor your cat's health, assess their overall well-being, and detect any issues early.
- By staying proactive with veterinary care, you can ensure your cat's long-term well-being and enjoy many happy and healthy years together.

27

Parasite prevention is crucial

Deworming

- Regular deworming treatments help eliminate intestinal parasites like roundworms, hookworms, and tapeworms.
- Discuss with your vet the appropriate deworming schedule based on your cat's age, lifestyle, and risk factors.
- Timely deworming ensures your cat's digestive system remains healthy and parasite-free.

Flea and Tick Prevention

- Fleas and ticks can transmit diseases and cause discomfort for your cat.
- Consult your veterinarian about safe and effective flea and tick prevention products suitable for your cat's age and size.
- Consistent use of preventive treatments protects your cat from infestations and reduces the risk of tick-borne illnesses.

28

Observe for abnormal behaviour

Eating and Drinking Habits

- Regularly observe your cat's appetite and water intake.
- Sudden changes, such as decreased or increased consumption, may signal underlying health issues.
- Any significant alterations in eating or drinking habits warrant prompt veterinary attention to rule out potential illnesses.

Sleeping Patterns

- Take note of your cat's sleeping routine and any deviations from the norm.
- Excessive lethargy or unusual sleep patterns could indicate illness or discomfort.

Play and Activity Levels

- Pay attention to your cat's playfulness and activity levels throughout the day.
- A sudden decrease in energy or interest in play may indicate illness or pain.
- Changes in behaviour during playtime should prompt a visit to the vet to address any underlying health issues and ensure your cat's well-being.

29

Pet insurance

Financial Safety Net

- Accidents, illnesses, or surgeries can be costly and pet insurance ensures your cat receives quality care without financial burden.
- Chronic or recurring issues like diabetes or allergies are usually covered, preventing financial strain over time.
- Difficult choices about treatment become less stressful knowing costs are managed.

Preventive Advantage

- Early detection of health problems is crucial and covered checkups keep your cat healthy and happy.
- Regular cleanings prevent serious dental issues, impacting their overall health and lifespan.
- Some insurance plans offer coverage for spaying/neutering, microchipping, even training.

Peace of Mind

- Knowing your beloved kitty is covered by insurance allows you to stay calm and focus on their recovery in case of an unfortunate issue, instead of the costs.

30

First-aid kit essentials

Tick Removal Tools

- Include fine-tipped tweezers in your first aid kit for safe and effective tick removal.
- Familiarize yourself with proper tick removal techniques to minimize the risk of disease transmission.
- Regularly check your cat for ticks, especially after outdoor activities, and promptly address any infestations.

Antiseptic Wipes and Cleaning Supplies

- Add antiseptic wipes to swiftly clean wounds or bites, reducing the risk of infection.
- Ensure your cleaning supplies are specifically formulated for cats, avoiding potential irritants.

Pet Thermometer

- Include a reliable pet thermometer for monitoring your cat's temperature during health concerns.
- Familiarize yourself with proper temperature-taking techniques to ensure accurate readings.

Chapter 6

Travel & Adventures

31

Stress-free car rides

Incremental Exposure

- Begin with short car rides, or even just sitting with your kitty in a stationary car, gradually increasing the duration as they become more accustomed.
- Slowly extend the rides, allowing your cat to adjust to the car's movement and sounds without feeling overwhelmed.

Create a Comfortable Environment

- Line the cat carrier with familiar bedding and place a few favourite toys inside to create a cozy and reassuring space.
- Maintain a comfortable temperature inside the car, avoiding extreme heat or cold.
- Use a calming pheromone spray or diffuser to promote relaxation during car journeys.

Remain Patient

- Reward your cat for calm behaviour during car rides with treats and affection.
- Remain consistent in your approach, allowing your cat to build confidence and associating car rides with happy outcomes over time.

32

Cat-friendly harness training

Early Introduction

- Begin harness training when your kitten is still young, increasing their acceptance.
- Choose a lightweight and adjustable harness suitable for a cat's size, allowing for a snug yet not restrictive fit.
- Gradually introduce the harness indoors, with treats, play, and gentle praise.

Reward Good Behaviour

- Reward your cat for wearing the harness, with treats and affection.
- Associate the harness with enjoyable activities, such as playtime, fostering the right attitude towards wearing it.

Gradual Outdoor Exposure

- Once your cat is comfortable with the harness indoors, venture into outdoor spaces.
- Choose quiet and secure locations, allowing your cat to explore at their own pace while still on the leash.

33

Cat-proofing your car

Secure Carrier Placement

- Place your cat in a sturdy and well-ventilated carrier, ensuring it's appropriately sized for comfort.
- Secure the carrier with seat belts to prevent movement during the car journey, minimizing stress and ensuring your cat's safety.
- Familiarize your cat with the carrier in advance, making it a comfortable space by using treats and soft bedding.

Avoid Distractions

- Remove any loose items inside the car that could pose a danger or create distractions.
- Minimize noise and sudden movements inside the car, creating a calm and stress-free environment for your cat.
- Ensure all windows and doors are securely closed, preventing chance of escape during stops or in case of accidental openings.

Take Breaks

- Plan for rest stops to attend to your cat's needs, offering water and reassurance, and keeping them safely contained in their carrier during breaks.

34

Backpack adventures

Cat-Specific Backpack

- Choose a backpack designed specifically for cats, ensuring it provides proper ventilation and security.
- Look for features like mesh windows, multiple entry points, and a comfortable interior to accommodate your cat.
- Opt for a backpack with adjustable straps and a secure harness attachment, to ensure your cat's safety, and to prevent escape.

Introduction to Backpacking

- Familiarize your cat with the backpack in a controlled, indoor environment before venturing outdoors.
- Place treats and familiar items inside the backpack, encouraging your cat to view it as a safe and enjoyable space.

Safe Outings

- Choose quiet and pet-friendly locations for your cat's first outdoor experiences.
- Monitor your cat's reactions to new stimuli, ensuring they feel secure and happy during outings.

Chapter 7

Dealing with Common Problems

35

Teething woes

Safe Chew Toys

- Introduce a variety of safe chew toys to redirect your kitten's teething instincts away from furniture.
- Opt for toys specifically designed for teething kittens, providing relief to their sore gums.
- Rotate chew toys regularly to maintain interest.

Teething Gels for Relief

- Consult your veterinarian for safe and vet-approved teething gels suitable for kittens.
- Apply teething gels to designated chew toys or surfaces, offering temporary relief from teething discomfort.

Chilled Comfort

- Offer a chilled, but not frozen, washcloth or a specially designed teething toy after placing it in the refrigerator.
- The cool sensation can soothe teething discomfort and provide a comforting experience for your kitten.

36

Scratching solutions

Scratch Posts

- Introduce scratch posts strategically placed in areas your cat frequents, providing an outlet for natural scratching behaviour.
- Opt for a variety of scratch posts, considering different textures to cater to your cat's preferences.
- Place scratch posts near favourite resting spots or in areas where your cat often stretches, encouraging them to use them.

Positive Reinforcement

- Reward your cat with treats or affection when they use the designated scratch posts, reinforcing the desired behaviour.
- Avoid scolding or punishing your cat for scratching furniture, as this may create stress and worsen the issue.

Use Catnip Effectively

- Apply catnip on scratch posts to attract your cat to these designated areas.
- The enticing aroma of catnip can make the scratch posts more appealing, diverting your cat's attention from furniture.
- Refresh catnip regularly to maintain its effectiveness.

37

Zoomies and play-aggression

Active Playtime Sessions

- Engage in regular play sessions to help your cat spend excess energy and reduce the frequency of zoomies.
- Schedule playtime before anticipated high-energy periods, like evenings, to proactively address playful aggression.

Stimulating Toys

- Puzzle feeders and treat-dispensing toys provide mental stimulation, contributing to a well-rounded play experience.
- Rotate toys regularly to maintain novelty, preventing boredom.

Implement Diversions

- Distract your cat with alternative activities when playful aggression emerges.
- Offer scratch posts or climbing structures to provide an outlet for natural behaviours and prevent excessive rough play.
- Reward moments of calm play and discourage overly aggressive behaviour to keep zoomies in check.

38

Night-time meows and annoyances

Consistent Sleep Schedule

- Establish a regular bedtime routine, including feeding and playtime, to signal to your cat that it's time for sleep.
- Consistency in sleep patterns helps regulate your cat's internal clock, promoting a more peaceful night for both of you.
- Avoid disrupting the schedule on weekends or holidays, where possible.

Create a Cozy Sleep Haven

- Designate a quiet, comfortable area with a cozy bed to encourage restful sleep.
- Choose a location away from high-traffic areas and loud noises to minimize disturbances during the night.
- Ensure the bed is appropriately sized and filled with soft bedding to cater to your cat's comfort preferences.

Ignore Attention-Seeking Meows

- Resist responding to night time meows that are attention-seeking and not due to distress.
- Ignoring these meows communicates that night time is for rest, discouraging disruptive behaviour.

39

Litter box woes

Maintain a Pristine Litter Box

- Regularly scoop and clean the litter box to provide a sanitary environment for your cat.
- Use unscented, clumping litter to appeal to your cat's preferences and make the box more inviting.
- Consider having multiple litter boxes in different locations to offer variety.

Consult with the Vet

- If your cat exhibits sudden or persistent litter box issues, consult your veterinarian to rule out underlying health concerns.
- Medical causes, such as urinary tract infections or gastrointestinal issues, may contribute to inappropriate toileting.

Praise them

- Reinforce good litter box behaviour by praising when they use it appropriately.
- Avoid punishment for accidents, as it may create stress and worsen the problem.

40

Respect your cat's boundaries

Observation is Key

- Pay close attention to your cat's body language and behaviour to identify signs of discomfort or stress.
- Notice subtle cues such as flattened ears, a twitching tail, or attempts to retreat for solitude.
- Respect their personal space by giving them the opportunity to unwind in a quiet, undisturbed area when needed.

Create Safe Zones

- Designate specific areas in your home where your cat can retreat for relaxation.
- Provide cozy hideaways or comfortable beds in these safe zones, ensuring your cat has a retreat option whenever they feel the need.
- Avoid interrupting or invading these spaces, reinforcing the idea that they have a secure and undisturbed retreat within the home.

Gradual Socialization

- Introduce social interactions gradually, allowing your cat to build trust at their own pace.
- Be mindful of your cat's mood and reactions, adjusting your approach to align with their comfort level.

Chapter 8

Level up your purr-ficiency

41

"Tail"-oring to your cat

The Tale of the Tail

- Observe the tail's height and movement to gauge your cat's mood.
- A raised tail indicates confidence and friendliness, while a lowered tail may signal fear or submission.
- Purring combined with an upright tail suggests a content and happy cat, ready for interaction.
- A cat wrapping its tail around you is a sign of affection and trust

Aggression

- A puffed-up tail signifies agitation or fear, indicating your cat feels threatened.
- If the tail is lashing or twitching rapidly, it may signal irritation or annoyance.
- Avoid approaching or touching your cat during these moments to prevent stress or potential aggression.

Give Space

- Respect your cat's signals; if the tail swishes or thumps, it might be a sign of overstimulation, and giving space is beneficial.

42

Extra care

Nail Trimming

- Utilize cat-specific nail clippers, cutting at a 45-degree angle to avoid splintering.
- Gradually introduce nail trimming, rewarding them and offering treats.
- If unsure, seek guidance from a veterinarian or professional groomer for hands-on training.

Bathing

- Choose cat-friendly shampoos and create a calm environment for a stress-free bath.
- Gently introduce water, starting with a damp cloth before progressing to full baths.
- Use treats, and soothing words to associate bathing as a safe experience.

Dental Care

- Regularly inspect your cat's teeth for tartar buildup, redness, or swelling.
- Gradually introduce tooth brushing using cat-specific toothpaste and a soft brush.
- Schedule professional dental check-ups to address any oral health concerns promptly.

AUTHOR BIO

Meet Deepak Panickal and Tina Joseph, a duo with a shared love for cats and a knack for ensuring their happiness. By day, Deepak delves into the world of software engineering, while Tina explores her creativity as an architect. Together, they call the vibrant city of Glasgow, Scotland, home sweet home, where they share their lives with their beloved cat, Mollykutty. With their adorable kitty by their side, Deepak and Tina bring a blend of expertise and affection to this book, offering fellow furball enthusiasts practical advice and insights for a purrfectly delightful journey alongside their feline friends.

Printed in Great Britain
by Amazon

40791181R00059